South Devon's Lost Railways

by
Peter Dale

Heathfield Station was on the Moretonhampstead branch and was the junction with the Teign Valley line from Exeter. The factory on the left produced tiles and pipes.

www.stenlake.co.uk

ISBN 1 84033 147 X

No. 4568 at Princetown Station which was on the Princetown branch. For most of its life this line was the preserve of 44XX 2-6-2Ts; only in later years did the 45XX class, such as this Prarie tank, make an appearance.

ACKNOWLEDGEMENTS

I would like to thank my father, who was a Devonian, for firing my interest in railways, and Ken Jones for introducing me to this project.

The publishers wish to thank the following for permission to reproduce the photographs in this book: John Alsop for the front cover, pages 1, 3–8, 10–17, 19–24, 26–30, 32–34 (both), 35, 38–48, and the inside back cover; W.A.C. Smith for the inside front cover and pages 9, 31 and 36; Neville Stead for pages 2, 18 and 25; and the Rev. D.J. Lane for page 37 and the back cover.

INTRODUCTION

Many people think of Devon, England's third largest county, as being synonymous with cream teas and holidays beside the sea. However, the county was an early participant in the Industrial Revolution as china clay and tin were found in commercial quantities in the west. Thomas Newcomen, the inventor of the first practical mechanical steam engine, hailed from Dartmouth and by 1800 over 1,000 of his type of engines were in use, although the more efficient Watt engine had appeared on the scene by then. One of the earliest railways in Devon, the Haytor Granite Tramway, opened in 1820 and blocks of the local stone it was built to carry were used for its tracks (and much of it can still be seen). Three years later the Plymouth & Dartmoor Railway opened using edge rails. Neither of these lines carried passengers.

South Devon was dominated by two pre-grouping companies, the London & South Western Railway (LSWR) and the Great Western Railway (GWR) which had absorbed the South Devon Railway (the lines of which were built to the broad gauge of 7 feet). The South Devon was of interest as services were intended to be operated not with locomotives but instead by powering vehicles with atmospheric pressure acting against a piston, in a tube between the rails, the other side of which was a partial vacuum. This partial vacuum was to be achieved by fixed pumping stations. However, it was not to be as the leather sealing valve caused constant trouble and conventional locomotives took over. A pumping station can still be seen at Starcross. Misplaced optimism as to the suitability of this system led to the steeply graded line still in use today between Plymouth and Newton Abbot.

Development of the area for holidaymakers came in the twentieth century, although many of Devon's resorts already had a history stretching back over a century to the Napoleonic Wars. The early 1900s also

brought the first road competition and both the GWR and the LSWR developed bus services, which were later sold off.

In 1923 the old railway companies were grouped into four. In Devon the LSWR became part of the Southern Railway, while the GWR continued. Despite increasing competition from road transport most lines continued through nationalisation in 1948 until the Beeching era.

The lines have been arranged in this book from west to east, starting with those in the Plymouth area. The narrative then moves along the GWR mainline, covering the various branches to Newton Abbot from where it follows a railway byway, the Teign Valley line, to get to Exeter. From Exeter it goes eastwards again along the ex-LSWR mainline, visiting the LSWR branches as far as the Lyme Regis line at Axminster.

It is hoped that the photographs in this book will revive pleasant memories of holidays by the sea for some and may encourage others to investigate what is left of our railway heritage.

The staff of Christow Station (which was on the Teign Valley line) with an 0-4-2T, no. 1440, which was built at Wolverhampton in 1877–78 as a member of the 517 class. In 1932 the 48XX class was introduced as a replacement for the 517s (this class was renumbered in the 14XX series in 1946).

Launceston branch *

Passenger service withdrawn	29 December 1962		
Distance	32 miles		
Company	South Devon Railway		

Stations closed	Date	Stations closed	Date
Marsh Mills	29 December 1962	Horrabridge	29 December 1962
Plym Bridge Halt	29 December 1962	Whitchurch Down Platform	29 December 1962
Bickleigh	29 December 1962	Tavistock South	29 December 1962
Shaugh Bridge Platform	29 December 1962	Mary Tavy & Blackdown	29 December 1962
Clearbrook Halt	29 December 1962	Lydford	29 December 1962
Yelverton	29 December 1962	Liddaton Halt	29 December 1962
		Coryton	29 December 1962
		Lifton	29 December 1962

* The closed station on this line that was in Cornwall was Launceston, the terminus.

Plym Bridge Halt served a local beauty spot
and traffic here could be intense on bank holidays.

Bickleigh Station was the first crossing place on the branch. Traffic to nearby Royal Marines bases required eight or nine coach trains at times.

This broad gauge line was originally promoted by the SDR as the South Devon & Tavistock Railway, partly to forestall the LSWR who had plans for a similar line, and opened in 1853 to Tavistock from a junction on the SDR mainline near Marsh Mills. The line was extended to Launceston by the Launceston & South Devon Railway in June 1865. In May 1876 LSWR trains began running on it, using a third rail, from Lydford to Plymouth and this continued until the LSWR got an independent route in June 1890. At first there were two companies and two stations at Lydford (with no junction between the railways after 1890), but from March 1914 the LSWR took over staffing of both, an arrangement which continued until 1962. One signal box had two lever frames, one for the GWR and the other for the LSWR, worked by one signalman. During the Second World War a junction was put in between the GWR and Southern lines at Lydford. The line was busy during the war years and immediately after as many people moved out of Plymouth to escape the heavy bombing the city suffered.

Yelverton Station. This was also the junction for the Princetown branch, the platform for which was behind the station building on the right.

Horrabridge Station around the turn of the twentieth century. The track appears to be broad gauge slewed into standard gauge. Note the wide gap between the platforms to accommodate two 7 feet gauge lines.

Whitchurch Down Station was staffed by one porter, under the stationmaster at Tavistock South, who issued tickets and kept it tidy.

An 0-6-0 pannier tank, no. 6413, at Tavistock South with the 2.10 p.m. push/pull train from Plymouth, August 1960.

A Launceston bound passenger train leaving Coryton Station. When the line opened there was a fair amount of manganese traffic from here.

CORYTON STATION.

256

Lifton Station derived much of its traffic from an adjacent dairy, although the picture shows the station before this was built.

Lifton Station.

Princetown branch

Passenger service withdrawn	5 March 1956	Stations closed	Date
Distance	10.5 miles	Dousland	5 March 1956
Company	Great Western Railway	Burra Tor Halt	5 March 1956
		Ingra Tor Halt	5 March 1956
		King Tor Halt	5 March 1956
		Princetown	5 March 1956

A 3101 class 2-6-2T departing from Princetown Station.

During the Napoleonic Wars a war prison was built in the bleakness of Dartmoor which kept French and, later, American prisoners of war. Princetown grew up around it. When peace returned the prison became disused with consequent economic decline for Princetown. In an effort to restore some prosperity to the area Sir Thomas Tyrwhitt proposed a railway, the Plymouth and Dartmoor, of about 25 miles in length to run from Plymouth to Princetown. This was built using what has been called the 'Dartmoor gauge' of 4 feet 6 inches. It opened in September 1823 and was horse worked. However, Princetown's fortunes only began to look up when the prison reopened as a civilian establishment in 1850. In 1877 the P&DR proposed the sale of its line from Yelverton to Princetown to a new company, the Princetown Railway Company. An agreement was made between the GWR and the P&DR that the GWR should work the line and have a controlling interest in it. A new standard gauge railway was built from a junction at Yelverton with the GWR line to Launceston, much of it on the trackbed of the P&DR and ironing out one or two of its worst contortions. It opened in August 1883. During the 1920s the GWR tried to encourage moorland walkers to use the line by opening two halts and a third one in the 1930s. Passenger traffic peaked in 1931. Much of this line across the moor can still be walked today.

Turnchapel branch

Passenger service withdrawn	10 September 1951	*Stations closed*	*Date*
Distance	2.2 miles	Lucas Terrace Halt	10 September 1951
Company	Plymouth & Dartmoor Railway	Plymstock	10 September 1951
		Oreston	10 September 1951
		Turnchapel	10 September 1951

An Adams 02 class 0-4-4T, no. 182, at Oreston Station, 1948.

This line was built under the auspices of the P&DR, a 4 feet 6 inch gauge line that had opened to Princetown in 1823, acting as the agent of the LSWR. It opened in September 1892. The line carried considerable suburban traffic but suffered from severe bus competition. It was closed in January 1951 when there was an energy shortage and although it reopened in July of that year, passenger levels did not recover and final closure soon followed.

An 02 class 0-4-4T at Turnchapel Station.

Yealmpton branch

		Stations closed	Date
Passenger service withdrawn	7 October 1947		
Distance	6.6 miles (Plymstock Junction to Yealmpton)	Billacombe	7 October 1947
Company	Great Western Railway	Elburton Cross	7 October 1947
		Brixton Road	7 October 1947
Stations closed	*Date*	Steer Point	7 October 1947
Mount Gould and Tothill Halt	1 February 1918	Yealmpton	7 October 1947

This line was originally promoted by the LSWR as the South Hams Railway, to leave the Turnchapel branch at Plymstock and run to Modbury. The GWR was concerned at possible competition from a future extension to Torbay and Exeter and an Act of 1894 transferred the rights for the section from Plymstock to Yealmpton to the GWR, while Yealmpton to Modbury remained with the LSWR. The GWR opened its part on 17 January 1898 with services running from Millbay, but the LSWR lost interest in the Modbury section and never exercised its running powers to Yealmpton. The GWR increased its service and the LSWR its Turnchapel service until Plymstock saw over sixty trains a day. The line was an early victim of road competition and closed in July 1930, reopening as a consequence of the war in 1941 with services running to and from Plymouth Friary.

Plymouth Friary

Passenger service withdrawn	15 September 1958	*Stations closed*	*Date*
Distance	1.6 miles (Lipson Junction to Friary)	Plymouth Friary	15 September 1958
Company	London & South Western Railway		

When the LSWR opened is own line through to Plymouth in 1890, its trains first shared Plymouth North Road Station with GWR trains (where LSWR and GWR London-bound trains could be seen leaving in opposite directions, a sight repeated at Exeter St Davids), but in May 1891 it opened its own terminus at Friary. This was also the terminus for Turnchapel and Yealmpton trains after 1941.

A 4-4-0, no. 113, at Plymouth Friary Station. This engine was a member of the famous T9 class (Greyhounds) built at Nine Elms in 1899–1900.

Devonport—St Budeaux

Passenger service withdrawn	7 September 1964	*Stations closed*	*Date*
Distance	2.8 miles	Camel's Head Halt	4 May 1942
Company	London & South Western Railway/Plymouth,	Ford	7 September 1964
	Devonport & South Western Junction Railway	Albert Road Halt	13 January 1947
		Devonport *	7 September 1964
Stations closed	*Date*		
Weston Mill Halt	27 June 1921	* Renamed as Devonport King's Road on 29 September 1949.	

When the LSWR first reached Plymouth in 1876, via the Tavistock branch of the GWR, its trains travelled over GWR lines through to Plymouth to reach its own terminus at Devonport. When the PD&SWJR line was completed from Lydford to give an independent route to Plymouth, it joined the LSWR at Devonport. This section was closed when the trains to Bere Alston were diverted over the GWR route to St Budeaux in 1964.

Devonport Stonehouse Pool

Passenger service withdrawn	1911	*Stations closed*	*Date*
Distance	1.2 miles	Devonport Stonehouse Pool	1911
Company	London & South Western Railway		

Opened in April 1904 for ocean liner traffic, the station is sometimes referred to as Plymouth Ocean Terminal or Ocean Quay.

Kingsbridge branch

Passenger service withdrawn	14 September 1963	*Stations closed*	*Date*
Distance	12.3 miles	Avonwick	14 September 1963
Company	Great Western Railway	Gara Bridge	14 September 1963
		Loddiswell	14 September 1963
		Kingsbridge	14 September 1963

Gara Bridge Station, looking towards Brent. This was the normal crossing point on the branch.

Loddiswell Station. Beyond the locomotive there was a loop and a goods yard.

This branch served the South Hams district of Devon from a junction with the GWR mainline at Brent. Many residents of the area were not in favour of a railway, Kingsbridge being served by three good coach services, and it was not until December 1893 that the line opened. When the GWR introduced camping coaches in 1934, Avonwick, Gara Bridge and Loddiswell all got such vehicles which were older coaches converted into holiday accommodation with lounges, kitchens and sleeping quarters (occupants were able to use the stations' toilets). A condition of booking these was that a certain number of full return fares were bought to encourage rail travel to and from the stations. The area was particularly important in the build-up to D-day and the railway saw correspondingly heavy traffic. Before the war the weekday Cornish Riviera Express carried a through coach for Kingsbridge which was detached at Exeter in the down direction and attached to the up train at Newton Abbot. At weekends the branch had its own through service to and from Paddington. Despite their indifference to the arrival of the railway, the people of the South Hams were not keen to see it go and efforts were made to save it, even to take it over as a preserved line. Sadly, these efforts were in vain.

No. 5544 waiting to depart from Kingsbridge Station in British Railways days.

Ashburton Branch

		Stations closed	Date
Passenger service withdrawn	1 November 1958	Staverton	1 November 1958
Distance	9.25 miles	Buckfastleigh	1 November 1958
Company	Buckfastleigh, Totnes & South Devon Railway	Ashburton	1 November 1958

Staverton Station, looking towards Buckfastleigh, 1921.

A 517 class approaching Buckfastleigh Station before the First World War. Note the posters advertising GWR services to Ireland and the Channel Islands.

The first proposal for a railway to Ashburton – the Ashburton, Newton & South Devon Railway – got no further than obtaining its Act in 1846. However, the line was promoted again in 1864 and was intended to run to Buckfastleigh, the extension to Ashburton being put forward in the following year. It opened as a broad gauge line on 1 May 1872, by which time Ashburton was already in decline, and was worked by the South Devon Railway from the beginning. Despite that about half of Devon's wool trade was in the Dart Valley and as late as 1890 Buckfastleigh provided more traffic than Newton Abbot. The local company was taken over by the GWR in 1897. It was normally worked by 14XX tanks and auto trailers, but did not serve any tourist resort and closed entirely in 1962. However, the section from Totnes (Riverside) to Buckfastleigh is now run by the South Devon Railway as a preserved line. Sadly, the section on to Ashburton was used for road improvements so trains no longer stop under Ashburton's all-over wooden roof which still stands.

Ashburton Station. The station building and roof is in the centre of the picture, while the goods shed is on the left.

Kingswear branch

Passenger service withdrawn	January 1973	*Stations closed*	*Date*
Distance	6.7 miles	Goodrington Sands	January 1973
Company	Dartmouth & Torbay Railway	Churston	January 1973
		Kingswear	January 1973

The Dartmouth & Torbay Railway was incorporated to extend the South Devon's Torre branch, first to Paignton and then to Churston (which was known as Brixham Road until the Brixham branch opened). Attempts to take trains to Dartmouth itself failed in the Lords, mainly due to the opposition of the landowner who would have been affected, and the line to Kingswear opened in August 1864. Ever since Dartmouth has been famous for, among other things, its station with no trains; a connection to Kingswear was provided by ferry across the River Dart. Although the line was single from Paignton, many trains, including the Torbay Express and trains to Birmingham and Manchester, worked through to Kingswear and there was a turntable at Kingswear to allow the locomotives to be turned. The line also had coal traffic from coasters calling at Kingswear. Since withdrawal of passenger services, the line has been operated as a tourist line in summer as the Paignton and Dartmouth Steam Railway.

Brixham branch

Passenger service withdrawn	13 May 1963	*Stations closed*	*Date*
Distance	2 miles	Brixham	13 May 1963
Company	Torbay & Brixham Railway		

This short broad gauge line opened in February 1868, making a junction with the South Devon Railway at Churston (which had previously been known as Brixham Road). It owed its existence to the efforts of a local solicitor, a Mr Wolston, who wanted to help his fishing port and even undertook the construction himself when the contractor defaulted. He let the SDR work the line as his agent but found that he was almost ruined by the line. It was then discovered that the SDR was not allowing him commission on traffic going beyond Churston. After two appeals were made to the Railway Commissioners, the SDR was forced to pay him £2,000. The GWR took over the SDR in 1876 and the Torbay and Brixham worked its own line until it too became part of the GWR in January 1883.

Moretonhampstead branch

Passenger service withdrawn	2 March 1959
Distance	12.2 miles
Company	Moretonhampstead
	& South Devon Railway

Stations closed	*Date*
Teigngrace	2 March 1959
Heathfield	2 March 1959
Bovey Tracey	2 March 1959
Lustleigh	2 March 1959
Moretonhampstead	2 March 1959

Bovey Tracey Station in the mid-1920s. On the right is a Burford forward control chassis fitted with a charabanc body, while on the left is an AEC 3½ ton chassis also fitted as a charabanc. There is another AEC in the background.

Lustleigh Station. The approaching train is headed by a GWR 0-6-0ST. Note the platelayers on the right.

Part of the trackbed of the Haytor Tramway, which used granite blocks as its rails, was used between Teigngrace and Bovey Tracey for this broad gauge line from Newton Abbot. It opened in July 1866 and was worked by the South Devon Railway from the outset. The line became popular as the resorts of the 'English Riviera' (Paignton and Torquay) grew. Moretonhampstead was a railhead for Dartmoor and by 1913 the GWR was running buses to Chagford and, in summer, 'automobile observation cars' (this was the term used for early charabancs) across the moor to Princetown.

Moretonhampstead Station. Only the first coach is a bogie one – the rest of the train is composed of four or six wheelers which would have been normal for a branch train in the early 1900s.

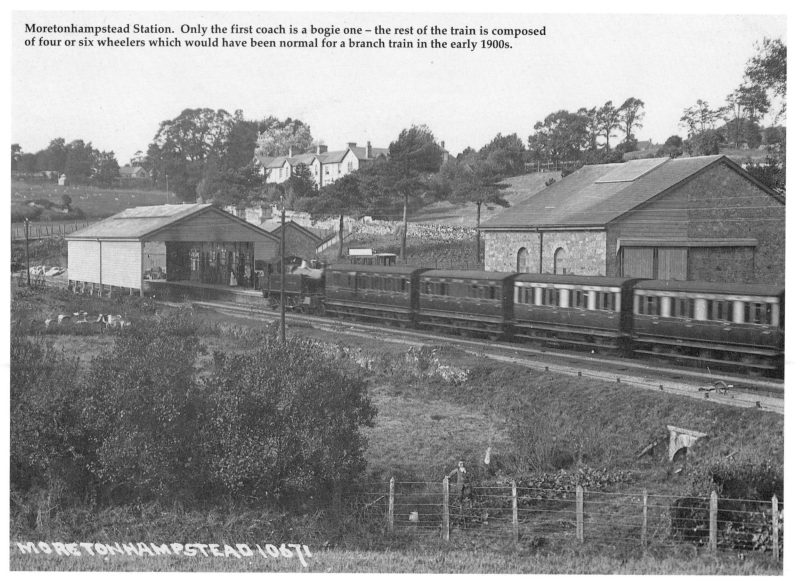

No. 5552 at Moretonhampstead, August 1953.

Teign Valley line

Passenger service withdrawn	9 June 1958	*Stations closed*	*Date*
Distance	15.8 miles	Trusham	9 June 1958
Company	Great Western Railway	Ashton	9 June 1958
		Christow	9 June 1958
Stations closed	*Date*	Longdown	9 June 1958
Chudleigh Knighton Halt	9 June 1958	Ide Halt	9 June 1958
Chudleigh	9 June 1958		

A 517 class 0-4-2T at Chudleigh Station. After 1923 the service was worked by railmotors and autotrains.

Trusham Station. At each end of the station there were sidings which gave access to quarries.

This line linked Heathfield to Exeter and was built in stages by two separate companies. The Teign Valley Railway (6.2 miles plus 1.5 miles for goods only) opened in October 1882 and ran from Chudleigh Road (later Heathfield) on the Moretonhampstead branch to Ashton, but no physical connection was possible until the end of the broad gauge in 1892 as it had been built as a standard gauge line. The line had a prolonged gestation, having been first proposed in 1863, but it made an enemy of the SDR when it proposed an extension to Exeter. There was a dalliance with the LSWR for a while and an extension to Crediton was planned. Eventually an agreement was reached with the GWR shortly before the line opened, having required no fewer than nine Acts of Parliament. The connection to Exeter City Basin Junction was only completed when the Exeter Railway opened in July 1903, 8.1 miles from Christow Junction. From this date the line was normally worked as a single entity and was a favourite haunt of steam railmotors and auto trains which worked from Exeter St Davids via St Thomas to join the branch.

Christow Station was the only crossing place on the line. An aerial ropeway carried stone the three quarters of a mile from the quarries to the railways.

When the GWR's coastal mainline was blocked the Teign Valley line acted as an alternative route for trains to Newton Abbot and the Torbay line but due to the awkward nature of the junction at Heathfield the Southern was the preferred route for diverted trains to Plymouth and Cornwall. Immediately after the Exeter Railway opened, plans were floated for a new mainline to use the Teign Valley as far as Heathfield with a new connection thence to Ashburton and another new section from Buckfastleigh to join the existing mainline at South Brent but nothing came of these plans. At one time the line carried a lot of roadstone traffic.

Ide Halt. The clothing of the people on the platform seems to indicate Edwardian times. It would be interesting to know if the constable was of the local force or a member of the railway police.

Sidmouth branch

Passenger service withdrawn	6 March 1967	*Stations closed*	*Date*
Distance	8.3 miles	Ottery St Mary	6 March 1967
Company	Sidmouth Railway	Tipton St Johns	6 March 1967
		Sidmouth	6 March 1967

Ottery St Mary Station, looking towards Sidmouth Junction. There was a passing loop and a goods yard here.

A class M7 0-4-4T, no. 30670, at Tipton St Johns with the 12.30 p.m. service to Sidmouth, August 1960.

The first railway in Sidmouth was built to assist in enclosing an area on the Esplanade. The locomotive was brought by sea to Exmouth and then pulled by teams of horses to Sidmouth, but the scheme came to naught and a lot of money was lost. Plans to link the town to the national network were put forward in the 1840s and '50s for both broad and narrow gauge lines, but it was July 1874 before the link from the mainline at Sidmouth Junction became a reality. It was worked by the LSWR from the outset, although the Sidmouth Railway retained its separate existence until 1923. The station was three quarters of a mile from the town and 200 feet above the beach, and it was rumoured that the distance of the station from the town was a deliberate attempt to discourage too many day trippers from lowering the tone of the place. Sidmouth was, in any case, on old-established resort, having been developed during the Napoleonic Wars when the Continent was out of bounds. The line was sufficiently important to run through coaches to Waterloo.

Sidmouth Station in LSWR days. The locomotive appears to be an 02 0-4-4T.

Railway Station, Sidmouth.

Budleigh Salterton Railway

Passenger service withdrawn	6 March 1967
Distance	10.9 miles
Company	Budleigh Salterton Railway

Stations closed	*Date*
Newton Poppleford	6 March 1967
East Budleigh	6 March 1967

Stations closed	*Date*
Budleigh Salterton	6 March 1967
Littleham	6 March 1967
Exmouth *	3 May 1976

* Replaced by a new station when the line was cut back by approximately 100 yards to make way for a roadway.

Newton Poppleford Station, June 1965. There was a goods siding here but that had been lifted by the time this picture was taken. When it opened Newton Poppleford had a stationmaster and a porter.

This line was opened in May 1897 from Tipton St Johns, on the Sidmouth branch, to Budleigh Salterton and was worked by the LSWR, which took over the local company in 1912. The extension to Exmouth was built by the LSWR and opened in June 1903 although Exmouth had previously been reached by the Exeter & Exmouth Railway in May 1861. In the 1920s the line had a service of ten trains through to Tipton St Johns and there were also a number of local services from Exmouth to Budleigh Salterton and back. Some trains followed a circular route: Exeter–Exmouth–Tipton St Johns–Sidmouth Junction–Exeter. Many through trains to Exmouth from Waterloo were worked over the branch, rather than the still extant line from Exeter. There were also through trains to more distant parts, including Nottingham and

Cleethorpes (both via the Somerset & Dorset Railway). Even today there is still the other, GWR, route to Exmouth – by train to Starcross and then ferry to Exmouth.

Budleigh Salterton (above) originally had only one platform but when the Exmouth extension opened a second one was added. The station came first in a 'Best Kept Station' competition fifteen times. Littleham Station (left) had a goods yard and a passing loop. There were usually at least two camping coaches here. Both of these photographs date from June 1965.

Seaton branch

Passenger service withdrawn	7 March 1966	Stations closed	Date
Distance	4.5 miles	Colyton *	7 March 1966
Company	Seaton & Beer Railway	Colyford	7 March 1966
		Seaton **	7 March 1966

Seaton Station in LSWR days.

* Originally named Colyton Town.   ** Originally named Seaton and Beer.

**A class M7 0-4-4T, no. 30045, at Seaton Station with the
3.46 p.m. service to Seaton Junction, August 1960.**

Built as an independent line which opened in March 1868, this became part of the LSWR in 1885. Like other towns on Devon's south coast, attempts were made to revive Seaton, which has no harbour, with tourism, but this was not helped by its largely shingle beach and having to compete with nearby resorts such as Lyme Regis and Sidmouth. Despite that, summer Saturdays could see as many as 500 holidaymakers arrive in the town and the line had through trains to Waterloo. Trains took 16 or 17 minutes for the journey and in Southern days were normally worked by M7 0-4-4Ts, but when the Southern Region lines west of Salisbury passed to the Western Region in 1963 it became the preserve of panniers and auto tanks. Since the line closed the trackbed between Colyford and Seaton has been used by the narrow gauge Seaton & District Electric Tramway which runs miniature passenger trams for a distance of 3 miles along it in the summer.

Lyme Regis branch *

Passenger service withdrawn   29 November 1965
Distance   6.8 miles
Company   Axminster & Lyme Regis Light Railway

Stations closed   Date
Combpyne   29 November 1965

* The closed station on this line that was in Dorset was Lyme Regis.

Nos. 30582 and 30584 near Combpyne with a service from Lyme Regis to Waterloo.

Opened in August 1903 this line was worked by the LSWR from the beginning. The 12 ton axle weight limit, the steep gradients and sharp curves on it made the choice of suitable motive power difficult and Terrier 0-6-0Ts, specially purchased from the London, Brighton & South Coast Railway, and 02 tanks with tanks half full were tried with only moderate success. It was only in 1913 that a solution was found, when it was decided to modify, with smaller water tanks, two Adams Radial tanks. This type had been introduced in 1882 and were already regarded as reserves and were liable for withdrawal within the near future. However, they remained the line's mainstay until 2-6-2Ts took over in the early 1960s. The line was at a disadvantage with a terminus about half a mile outside Lyme Regis and 250 feet above it. Its main engineering work was the ten arch concrete viaduct at Cannington. The line became part of the LSWR in 1907.

Closed passenger stations on lines still open to passengers

Line/service	Great Western Railway mainline	Station closed	Date
		Ivybridge **	2 March 1959
		Bittaford Platform	2 March 1959
Station closed	Date	Wrangaton ***	2 March 1959
Ford Halt	6 October 1941	Brent	5 October 1964
Wingfield Villas Halt	June 1921	Exminster	30 March 1964
Mutley	3 July 1939	Stoke Canon ****	13 June 1960
Lipson Vale Halt	22 March 1942	Silverton	5 October 1964
Laira Halt	7 July 1930	Hele and Bradninch	5 October 1964
Laira *	4 April 1849	Cullompton	5 October 1964
Plympton	2 March 1959	Burlescombe	5 October 1964
Cornwood	2 March 1959		

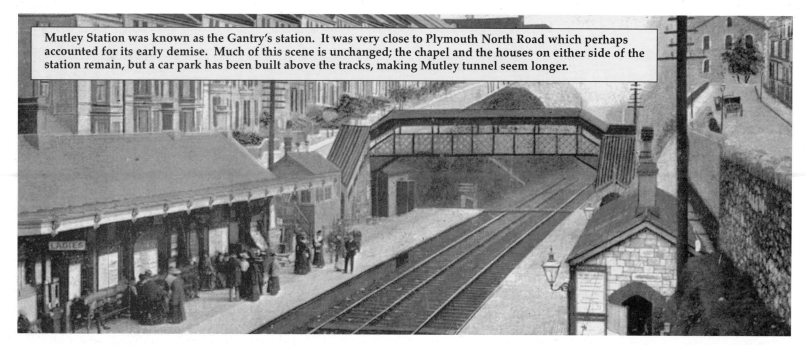

Mutley Station was known as the Gantry's station. It was very close to Plymouth North Road which perhaps accounted for its early demise. Much of this scene is unchanged; the chapel and the houses on either side of the station remain, but a car park has been built above the tracks, making Mutley tunnel seem longer.

* This was a temporary station opened in May 1848, prior to Millbay which was also known as Laira Green.
** Reopened 15 July 1994.

*** Renamed Kingsbridge Road in 1849; reverted to Wrangaton, 1 July 1895.
**** In July 1894 this replaced an earlier station that stood 400 metres north.

Plympton Station. At one time railmotors ran here as part of the Plymouth suburban service, but they were withdrawn in 1930.

A 4-4-0 with a down train at Bittaford Platform. A short distance west of here was the transhipment siding for the 3 feet gauge Redlake Tramway which carried clay.

A 4-4-0, probably Duke class, entering Brent Station with an up train, *c.*1907.

Another up train at Brent, probably between 1908 and 1922. The branch platform is on the left.

Silverton Station, June 1965. There was an accident near here in May 1876 when the first coach of the down 'Flying Dutchman' left the rails at 60 miles per hour. Fortunately there were no fatalities.

SILVERTON

Hele & Bradninch Station, looking towards Exeter.
There was a goods shed, cattle dock and coal yard here.

Cullompton Station. In the early 1930s the line here was quadrupled to ease congestion and the platforms were served by loops.

Line/service

Torbay line

Station
Kingskerswell
Preston Platform

Date of closure
5 October 1964
21 September 1914

Kingskerswell Station, around 1900. Note the signal above the bridge; signals were sited like this to improve their visibility for locomotive crews.

Line/service		LSWR mainline	Station	Date of closure
			Broad Clyst	7 March 1966
Station		Date of closure	Sidmouth Junction *	6 March 1967
Whipton Bridge Halt		1 January 1923	Seaton Junction	7 March 1966
Mount Pleasant Halt		2 January 1928		

* Reopened as Feniton, 5 May 1971.

Broad Clyst Station, June 1965. The station kept its gas lamps to the end and the last steam working from Exmouth Junction shed was about a month earlier.